Dream
Big
TALK
Big

& Turn Your Faith Loose!

Kenneth Copeland

KENNETH
COPELAND
PUBLICATIONS

Unless otherwise noted, all scripture is from the *King James Version* of the Bible.

Scripture quotations marked *The Amplified Bible* are from *The Amplified Bible, Old Testament* © 1965, 1987 by the Zondervan Corporation. *The Amplified New Testament* © 1958, 1987 by The Lockman Foundation. Used by permission.

Dream Big, Talk Big, and Turn Your Faith Loose

ISBN 978-1-60463-208-8   30-0075

21 20 19 18 17 16   7 6 5 4 3 2

Kenneth Copeland Publications
Fort Worth, TX 76192-0001

For more information about Kenneth Copeland Ministries, visit kcm.org or call 1-800-600-7395 (U.S. only) or +1-817-852-6000.

DREAM
Big
TALK
Big
& Turn Your Faith Loose!

If we really got honest with ourselves, most of us would probably admit that we haven't been receiving from heaven the way we could and should.

The Bible is packed full of promises of BLESSING from God. But how many of them are real to us? How many of them do we see fully manifesting in our daily lives?

That's not to say we couldn't use a miracle or two to help us out of a financial problem, health problem or marriage problem, right now. Miracles are wonderful manifestations of God's love, and they are for us.

But shouldn't there be more to this life in God than waiting for Him to bail us out of a tight spot with another miracle?

Let's face it. We've not been walking in the fullness of our covenant rights. I know it. You know it. God knows it. Even the devil knows it, but he's the only one happy about it.

Somehow, we've been missing out on *all* God has for us in this lifetime, and it's time for that to change.

Better Than a Miracle?

Let me say it this way: God never intended for us to keep our finances in line through the working of miracles. He never intended for us to live in healthy bodies by the gifts of healings. He never intended for us to get up every morning and plan the activities of our day based on words of prophecy.

God's plan for every aspect of our lives was, is, and always will be for us to live by His every WORD (Deuteronomy 8:3; Luke 4:4). He intended for us to eat, sleep and breathe by faith—faith in every WORD that comes from His mouth.

That's not to say that miracles don't have their place. They do. Yet, there has been a gross lack of understanding about their purpose. God gave the gifts of the Spirit to the Church so we could minister to unbelievers. He also gave these gifts as signs to confirm His WORD.

Now, granted, any manifestation of God in this earth would seem miraculous to us because we live in a natural world. Everything God does is supernatural. Nonetheless, God fully intended for His people to live on the same supernatural level as He does.

How?

By what the Apostle Peter called the *more sure Word*.

More sure than what? Reporting his own eyewitness account of a sign and wonder, Peter wrote:

For we have not followed cunningly devised fables...but were eyewitnesses of his majesty. For [Jesus] received from God the Father honour and glory, when there came such a voice to him from the excellent glory, This is my beloved Son, in whom I am well pleased. And this voice which came from heaven we heard, when we were with him in the holy mount. We have also a more sure word of prophecy... (2 Peter 1:16-19).

In Matthew's account of this same supernatural manifestation of God, it's interesting to note that Jesus told Peter, James and John, "Tell the vision to no man..." (Matthew 17:9). Jesus called their experience a *vision.*

In this vision, Peter and the others watched as Jesus spoke face to face with Moses and Elijah, and they actually heard the audible voice of God. Now that's a vision!

But it's even more interesting that in other biblical accounts of God speaking in an audible voice, people did not agree on what they heard. Many said it thundered. Others said they heard the voice of an angel. That's to say, there was confusion as to what really happened.

Now there is no denying that physical manifestations of God's presence and power can be spectacular to our natural senses, but in dealing with the audible voice of God, or with visions or dreams, there is often some degree of uncertainty. Because of that, our lives could end up being very uncertain if we continually tried to live on something we *thought* we heard God say, or something we *thought* He gave us in a dream.

God never promised that we would have physical manifestations or audible words from heaven. While they are real, and they are available to us, they only come as the Spirit of God wills, not as we will.

What are we guaranteed, then?

Peter went on to say, "We have also a *more sure word* of prophecy; whereunto ye do well that ye take heed, as unto a light that shineth in a dark place, until the day dawn, and the day star arise in your hearts" (2 Peter 1:19).

Prophecy is a supernaturally spoken word in a known language that brings edification, exhortation and comfort. The disciples heard a supernaturally spoken word from God. It was the audible voice of Almighty God. And yet, Peter said, "We have a more sure word." Not, "as sure." But, "more sure."

That more sure word to which he was referring is the written WORD of God.

Cover-to-Cover God

I was studying about this "more sure word" when I heard the voice of the Spirit say, *This Book is not* about *Somebody. This Book is Somebody.*

Think about that for a moment.

John 1:1 says, "In the beginning was The WORD, and The WORD was with God, and The WORD was God." God and The WORD are One and the same. They cannot be separated.

But now, notice this: "And The WORD [or God] was made flesh, and dwelt among us, (and we beheld his glory, the glory as of the only begotten of the Father,) full of grace and truth" (John 1:14).

The WORD—God—became flesh among us. It—He—came alive (see Hebrews 4:12), and was full of grace and truth. Notice the word *truth*.

Jesus, in praying for His disciples in John 17:17, said, "Thy WORD is truth."

So we see that *God, The WORD* and *Truth* are all One. They are the same.

When Jesus lived and ministered on this earth, He walked according to the written WORD of God. He literally lived by The WORD, or by the truth, as His Father taught Him. He didn't have a free ride because He was the Son of God. He didn't live from miracle to miracle.

No, Jesus walked by faith in His Father's more sure WORD.

That's good news for us because if Jesus could live life to its fullest by walking by faith in The WORD of God, so can we.

In fact, when Jesus appeared to His disciples after having been raised from the grave, He told Thomas, "Because thou hast seen me, thou hast believed: blessed are they that have not seen, and yet have believed" (John 20:29).

Thomas had already been told by the others that Jesus had indeed risen from the dead, but he didn't believe them. Jesus Himself had told Thomas and the other disciples several times that He would rise again on the third day. Then there were all the writings of the prophets telling of Jesus' resurrection from the dead.

The point is, Thomas had plenty of WORD on the matter. Still, his attitude was, "If I don't see a sign or wonder of God myself, then I won't believe."

Well, Jesus didn't say, *Blessed are those who receive a miracle from heaven and believe.* He said, *BLESSED are they who see no signs or wonders, and yet believe. BLESSED are those who walk by faith in the more sure WORD My Father has given.*

How much more WORD did Thomas need?

How much more WORD do we need?

There are things we cannot see, but that does not mean they're not real. Your body may be telling you that you're not healed, but God's WORD says you are. Your creditors may be telling you that you're not debt free, but God's WORD says you are.

So it's simply a matter of getting those things we cannot see over to where we can see them, which is where faith comes in. Hebrews 11:1 tells us that "faith is the substance of things hoped for, the evidence of *things not seen.*"

You and I don't have to wait for a miracle. We have the opportunity to lay hold of Almighty God any moment of any hour of any day, and without any uncertainty. We can do it through His WORD. It's here. It's real. And it's literally God Himself. It's God talking to us.

Faith, then, comes by hearing that more sure WORD of God (Romans 10:17).

When we listen to The WORD, when we listen to Him talking to us—and then we talk it, we think it, we dream it and we do it—faith will rise up. Faith will rise up and lay hold of those things in the supernatural realm, which cannot be seen, and it will draw them into this natural realm.

When the supernatural manifestation of God's BLESSING becomes real in our everyday lives, to people around us, it will look like a miracle. But to us, it's just a way of life...it's just the way of faith.

Dream BIG...Talk BIG...

Imagine, now, having enough faith to impress God.

Does that seem a little far-fetched?

In Matthew 8, a centurion, a commanding officer of the Roman army, came to Jesus on behalf of his servant who was sick and tormented.

When Jesus offered to go to the centurion's home and heal his servant, the officer said, "Lord, I am not worthy that thou shouldest come under my roof: but speak the *word* only, and my servant shall be healed" (verse 8).

Now here was a man who understood the power of words. He was, after all, an army officer. When he spoke, everyone listened—and then they did what he said.

In this case, so did Jesus.

Why was Jesus so quick to respond? Because the man's words were full of faith.

In fact, when Jesus heard the centurion's reply, He was astonished, and said, "I tell you truly, I have not found so much faith as this with anyone, even in Israel" (verse 10, *The Amplified Bible*).

The faith that so impressed Jesus was the centurion's willingness to believe without requiring a spectacular sign or wonder from heaven. All he needed in order to believe that Jesus could heal his servant was The WORD.

"Speak the word only," he said. And within the hour his servant was healed.

Who Needs a Miracle…?

That same faith and greater—faith that impresses God—is available to every one of us through God's WORD. God sent His WORD to heal us. He sent it to deliver us (Psalm 107:20). The WORD became flesh—in the person of Jesus— and lived among us. In Him, in God, in The WORD, is life, and that life is our light (John 1:1-14; Psalm 119:105).

The Bible is literally God talking to each one of us—which takes us back to why Peter called The WORD of God the *more sure word.*

Remember, miracles don't happen every day. They are an act of God's will, not ours. So we shouldn't try to live from miracle to miracle. God never intended it to be that way. He never promised a daily dose of visions, dreams, prophecies and miracles for us to live by.

What God did provide, however, was a book full of living promises. He sent His WORD. He gave us a book overflowing with life. He gave us a book overflowing with Himself.

Peter went on to say, "Ye do well that ye take heed [to the written WORD], as unto a light that shineth in a dark place, until the day dawn, and the day star arise in your hearts" (2 Peter 1:19).

In other words, you may not wake up and hear the audible voice of God every morning, but you do have His WORD. You have His promises, His revelation, His wisdom—and it's all as sure as the sun rising every day. So live by it.

Yes, miracles are wonderful. But God's plan is for us to walk by faith, not by sight (2 Corinthians 5:7). He expects us to live each day by faith in His WORD, not by the signs and wonders we might see along the way.

May I Have That in Writing?

Think for just a moment about one

of the great Old Testament examples we have of walking by faith and not by sight—Abraham.

When God called Abraham out of his homeland, telling him to leave his family and go to a new land, there was no *written* WORD of God. There wasn't even an Old Covenant. All Abraham had to go on was a spoken promise.

"Get thee out of thy country," God had told him. "And I will make of thee a great nation" (Genesis 12:1-2).

At the time, *Abram* was 75 years old and married to a barren woman. Yet, he took God at His WORD and left his family and homeland behind.

When Abram finally arrived in Canaan, God appeared to him and said,

"Unto thy seed will I give this land" (Genesis 12:7). Then, in Genesis 13, God told him, "All the land which thou seest, to thee will I give it, and to thy seed for ever. And I will make thy seed as the dust of the earth..." (verses 15-16).

The point is, all along the way, God kept speaking the promise and speaking the promise.

But in Genesis 15:2, after God had appeared to him in a vision, Abram asked God, "What wilt thou give me, seeing I go childless?"

At this point, Abram had given in to the circumstances. He was 86, and day after day all he had been *seeing* was a barren wife and no child. He complained even more by saying, "Behold, to me thou hast given no seed" (verse 3).

The truth was God had given Abram *seed*. He just didn't realize it. From the very beginning, God had given him His WORD—and the living WORD of God is seed (Mark 4).

I will make you a great nation...I will give this land to your seed...I will make your seed as the dust of the earth. God had spoken all that to Abram in the span of 11 years. Still, Abram was having trouble anchoring his faith in God's WORD. So God gave him a little help.

First, God took Abram out into the night and challenged him to count the stars. *So shall thy seed be,* He told him. And Abram believed (Genesis 15:5).

Then God cut covenant with Abram

using animal sacrifices, which was a sign to him that God would keep His promise. This blood covenant was a powerful anchor for Abram's faith. Yet 13 years later—at the age of 99—Abram still had no child.

That's when God began putting The WORD into Abram's mouth.

New Identity—New Destiny

From the moment God first told Abram that He would make him a great nation, Abram could have said, "OK, from now on I'm going to call myself *Abraham*, because God has said I will be the father of many nations. And if God said it—and I agree with it—then it is!"

Abram could have done that and

saved himself a lot of trouble. But he didn't. Remember, Abram was not born again or spiritually alive like us, and there was no written WORD for him to keep before his eyes. Consequently, all he was *seeing* was, "I am childless and have no seed." God fixed that, too, by changing his name.

When *Abram* became *Abraham*, he literally took on the new identity of "father of many nations"—which was what his new name meant. Every time he said his name, he was saying, "Hello, I'm the father of many nations." What's more, every time someone called his name, they were saying, "Hey, father of many nations!"

What was happening? Abraham and everyone around him was calling "those things which be not as though they were" (Romans 4:17). In effect, Abraham was speaking the same WORD God had spoken, and he was hearing it spoken as well.

Jesus did the same thing with Peter. When Jesus first met Peter, his name was Simon Barjona. Later, however, Jesus changed it to Peter, *the Rock*. And if there were anyone among the disciples who was not a "rock," it was Peter.

Jesus knew what He was doing. He called Peter *Rock* until he became one. Meanwhile, by receiving his new name and speaking it and responding to it, Peter was actually agreeing with The WORD of God. He was agreeing with The WORD that Jesus had spoken to him.

So, we see that the process behind

these name changes, and men fulfilling their destinies by agreeing with what God said they would be and do, was actually meditating The WORD— speaking it and hearing it, over and over and over.

Meditating The WORD was also the plan for success that God laid out for Joshua when he stepped into the role of leading all of Israel after Moses died. "This book of [My WORD] shall not depart out of thy mouth," God told him, "but thou shalt *meditate* therein day and night, that thou [may be able to see] to do according to all that is written therein: for then thou shalt make thy way prosperous, and then thou shalt have good success" (Joshua 1:8).

The Hebrew word we translate as

meditate actually means "to mutter or to go around talking to yourself." In short, Joshua was promised good success if he went through life constantly talking God's WORD—speaking it to himself, speaking it to others, and speaking it in every situation.

Can You Imagine?

When Abraham finally received by faith that he was, indeed, the father of many nations, it still wasn't something he could see with his physical eyes. So how did he see it?

In Psalm 2:1 *(The Amplified Bible),* we find that the word *meditate* can also mean "to imagine." The idea is, as we go about like Abraham, Joshua and Peter, constantly speaking God's WORD—calling those things that be not as though they were—The WORD will spark an inner image within us. That inner image in turn becomes hope, and hope is where Abraham saw himself as "father of many nations."

I remember in the early days of this ministry when Gloria and I reached the point where we needed a station wagon to get us and our children from one place to the next so I could preach. Like anything else we needed, we went to God's promises concerning our need, then we prayed, sowed seed, believed God and started speaking The WORD. That's what we did for that car.

After we had taken The WORD and agreed as a family in faith, we went around saying, "Glory to God for our new car!" "That new car is ours!" "Thank God for our new car!" We continued to meditate The WORD. At the time, our children were young, but still old enough to grab hold of our station wagon with their faith, too.

One day our son, John, asked, "Daddy, is that new car ours?"

"You bet it is," I replied.

"Well, let's go get it," he said.

This new car idea had become so real and so big inside him that he didn't see why we shouldn't just go get it. I didn't tell him that the reason we didn't go get the car was because we were $3,000 short of what we needed to buy it. In fact, I started to say, "Now, you know, John, we do have to...." But then I stopped, because I realized I was about to head down the road of doubt and unbelief.

Instead, I said, "Yeah, praise God! Let's do, John. Let's just go get it!"

Immediately we all started saying it to each other: "Let's go get it!"

In less than a week, a man called me, crying. "Oh, Brother Copeland, I'm so ashamed of myself. God told me to send you $3,000 a few days ago and I didn't do it. I've hung on to it until I cannot stand it anymore." The first time that man heard God tell him to send us the money was the same time John came to me and said, "Let's go get it!"

So we went and got it.

Wishing Wells Run Dry

The bottom line to all of this is that real Bible hope is not *wishing* for something to come to pass. God is not sitting at the bottom of a wishing well, waiting for us to toss in a few pennies so He can work up a miracle on our behalf.

No, hope is a divine inner image. It's a dream birthed by The WORD of God in the soul of man. It's the blueprint of our faith.

Hebrews 11:1 tells us that hope is what faith must have in order to bring our dreams to pass. We're told that it's also "an anchor of the soul, both sure and stedfast" (Hebrews 6:19).

So not only do we have a more sure word of prophecy, but we also have a sure hope. It's like Peter said: The

WORD of God—God's promises—enters our lives bringing light to the circumstances we face (2 Peter 1:19). As we meditate on The WORD, the light of it becomes brighter and brighter. It grows and develops on the inside of us, eventually giving birth to an inner image of what we're believing to receive from God.

In the past we may have seen ourselves as Abram saw himself—*childless.* We may have seen ourselves as moneyless, sick, desperate or whatever. But once we lay hold of The WORD, realizing that it is God Himself speaking directly to us, we give place to hope—and that hope gives life to the dreams God has placed within us.

Abraham hoped against hope

(Romans 4:18). He went against all the odds. We can too.

Receive God's WORD for your situation, right now. Receive the seed God has for your life. Then begin speaking it, hearing it, muttering it. Meditate The WORD until you begin *seeing* it...and dreaming it.

Go ahead—dream BIG. Talk BIG. And turn your faith loose!

Prayer for Salvation and Baptism in the Holy Spirit

Heavenly Father, I come to You in the Name of Jesus. Your Word says, "Whosoever shall call on the name of the Lord shall be saved" (Acts 2:21). I am calling on You. I pray and ask Jesus to come into my heart and be Lord over my life according to Romans 10:9-10: "If thou shalt confess with thy mouth the Lord Jesus, and shalt believe in thine heart that God hath raised him from the dead, thou shalt be saved. For with the heart man believeth unto righteousness; and with the mouth confession is made unto salvation." I do that now. I confess that Jesus is Lord, and I believe in my heart that God raised Him from the dead. I repent of sin. I renounce it. I renounce the devil and everything he stands for. Jesus is my Lord.

I am now reborn! I am a Christian—a child of Almighty God! I am saved! You also said in Your Word, "If ye then, being evil, know how to give good gifts unto your children: HOW MUCH MORE shall your heavenly Father give the Holy Spirit to them that ask him?" (Luke 11:13). I'm also asking You to fill me with the Holy Spirit. Holy Spirit, rise up within me as I praise God. I fully expect to speak with other tongues as You give me the utterance (Acts 2:4). In Jesus' Name. Amen!

Begin to praise God for filling you with the Holy Spirit. Speak those words and syllables you receive—not in your own language, but the language given to you by the Holy Spirit. You have to use your own voice. God will not force you to speak. Don't be concerned with how it sounds. It is a heavenly language!

Continue with the blessing God has given you and pray in the spirit every day.

You are a born-again, Spirit-filled believer. You'll never be the same!

Find a good church that boldly preaches God's Word and obeys it. Become part of a church family who will love and care for you as you love and care for them.

We need to be connected to each other. It increases our strength in God. It's God's plan for us.

Make it a habit to watch the *Believer's Voice of Victory Network* television broadcast and become a doer of the Word, who is blessed in his doing (James 1:22-25).

About the Author

Kenneth Copeland is co-founder and president of Kenneth Copeland Ministries in Fort Worth, Texas, and best-selling author of books that include *Honor—Walking in Honesty, Truth and Integrity*, and *THE BLESSING of The LORD Makes Rich and He Adds No Sorrow With It*.

Since 1967, Kenneth has been a minister of the gospel of Christ and teacher of God's WORD. He is also the artist on award-winning albums such as his Grammy-nominated *Only the Redeemed*, *In His Presence*, *He Is Jehovah*, *Just a Closer Walk* and *Big Band Gospel*. He also co-stars as the character Wichita Slim in the children's adventure videos *The Gunslinger*, *Covenant Rider* and the movie *The Treasure of Eagle Mountain*, and as Daniel Lyon in the Commander Kellie and the Superkids™ videos *Armor of Light* and *Judgment: The Trial of Commander Kellie*. Kenneth also co-stars as a Hispanic godfather in the 2009 and 2016 movies *The Rally* and *The Rally 2: Breaking the Curse*.

With the help of offices and staff in the United States, Canada, England, Australia, South Africa, Ukraine and Latin America Kenneth is fulfilling his vision to boldly preach the uncompromised WORD of

God from the top of this world, to the bottom, and all the way around. His ministry reaches millions of people worldwide through daily and Sunday TV broadcasts, magazines, teaching audios and videos, conventions and campaigns, and the World Wide Web.

Learn more about Kenneth Copeland Ministries by visiting our website at **kcm.org.**

When the Lord first spoke to Kenneth and Gloria Copeland about starting the *Believer's Voice of Victory* magazine...

He said: *This is your seed. Give it to everyone who ever responds to your ministry, and don't ever allow anyone to pay for a subscription!*

For more than 50 years, it has been the joy of Kenneth Copeland Ministries to bring the good news to believers. Readers enjoy teaching from ministers who write from lives of living contact with God, and testimonies from believers experiencing victory through God's Word in their everyday lives.

Today, the *BVOV* magazine is mailed monthly, bringing encouragement and blessing to believers around the world. Many even use it as a ministry tool, passing it on to others who desire to know Jesus and grow in their faith!

Request your FREE subscription to the
***Believer's Voice of Victory* magazine today!**

Go to **freevictory.com** to subscribe online, or call us at
1-800-600-7395 (U.S. only) or **+1-817-852-6000**.

We're Here for You!®

Your growth in God's Word and your victory in Jesus are at the very center of our hearts. In every way God has equipped us, we will help you deal with the issues facing you, so you can be the **victorious overcomer** He has planned for you to be.

The mission of Kenneth Copeland Ministries is about all of us growing and going together. Our prayer is that you will take full advantage of all The LORD has given us to share with you.

Wherever you are in the world, you can watch the *Believer's Voice of Victory* broadcast on television (check your local listings), the internet at kcm.org or on our digital Roku channel.

Our website, **kcm.org,** gives you access to every resource we've developed for your victory. And, you can find contact information for our international offices in Africa, Australia, Canada, Europe, Latin America, Ukraine and our headquarters in the United States.

Each office is staffed with devoted men and women, ready to serve and pray with you. You can contact the worldwide office nearest you for assistance, and you can call us for prayer at our U.S. number, +1-817-852-6000, seven days a week!

We encourage you to connect with us often and let us be part of your everyday walk of faith!

Jesus Is LORD!

Kenneth & Gloria Copeland

Kenneth and Gloria Copeland